INFORMATION IN SMALL BITS

First published and distributed by the Information Theory Society of IEEE
via CreateSpace, as part of the Claude Shannon centennial celebration.

 ieee.org

Story by Anna Scaglione and Christina Fragouli
Original illustrations by Anna Scaglione

Design, colors, production and art direction by Dawn Faelnar
for the Information Theory Society of IEEE.

DK Lemon Yellow Sun font by Hanoded Type Foundry.

INFORMATION IN SMALL BITS
© 2017 by the Information Theory Society of IEEE (Institute of Electrical and Electronics Engineers)
Copyright on text, illustrations, and design work (including the characterizations of Dr. Claude Shannon, Alice, Bob, and Eve) in this book are held by respective contributors. All Rights Reserved.
No part of this book may be reproduced in any form or by any electronic or mechanical means including information storage and retrieval systems without permission in writing from a representative of the Information Theory Society of IEEE (Institute of Electrical and Electronics Engineers) except by a reviewer, who may quote brief passages in a review.

All artwork and textual information in this book are based on the materials offered by the designers and contributors whose work have been included. While every effort has been made to ensure their accuracy, the Information Theory Society of IEEE, its designers, and affiliates do not accept any responsibility for any errors or omissions under any circumstances.

The authors gratefully acknowledge support from the National Science Foundation over the years. While this book project may not have been the direct goal of our research grants, one cannot dissociate it from the emphasis on outreach and education that the National Science Foundation imbues on its awardees.

ISBN 978-1979902977

I JUST WONDERED HOW THINGS WERE PUT TOGETHER.

~ CLAUDE SHANNON

CHAPTER 01
SIGNALS TO BITS

WHEN WE HUMANS WRITE A STORY, we use letters. The letters are our basic symbols, and we use them to compose words and express what we want to say. We write our stories on paper to remember them or give them to other people to read. Reading and writing is how information can last over time and is remembered and passed generation through generation.

Well, you probably are already writing all kind of things on all kind of computers, tablets, phones. That is not paper! How does that really work? What kind of people worked on this new "paper?"

In the last century, many brilliant electrical engineers came up with a new method that created all of these wonderful gadgets that your Mom is worried you play too much with. The computers, cellphones, and robots have tiny crystals in their memory—each little crystal can be made to either be "full" or "empty" of something called "electrical charge," like cells in a beehive that can either have honey or be empty.

We can use each little crystal to store what is called one "bit" that takes value either zero or one: when a little crystal is full it holds the value one, and when it is empty, it holds the value zero.

A <u>BIT</u> is the smallest amount of information we can have. We can think of a bit as the answer to a yes or no question. If someone asks you: "do you like cake?" and you answer yes or no, we can store your answer in a computer using 1 bit: we can store the value "one" if you answered "yes" and the value "zero" if you answered "no."

BUT HOW CAN WE USE BITS TO WRITE HUMAN WORDS?

If you write the sentence "I saw a whale" on your screen, your computer—in order to store it—needs to have a way to map the letters that you used to bits, to zeros and ones.

WE CAN DO THIS USING A <u>CODE</u>.

A code maps a different group of bits to each letter so that later, one can read this group of bits back from the memory of the computer and know which letter your wrote. This is what happens instantly when you push a key in a computer. One code that engineers use is the ASCII (American Standard Code for Information Interchange) code:

a	01100001	A	01000001	n	01101110	N	01001110
b	01100010	B	01000010	o	01101111	O	01001111
c	01100011	C	01000011	p	01110000	P	01010000
d	01100100	D	01000100	q	01110001	Q	01010001
e	01100101	E	01000101	r	01110010	R	01010010
f	01100110	F	01000110	s	01110011	S	01010011
g	01100111	G	01000111	t	01110100	T	01010100
h	01101000	H	01001000	u	01110101	U	01010101
i	01101001	I	01001001	v	01110110	V	01010110
j	01101010	J	01001010	w	01110111	W	01010111
k	01101011	K	01001011	x	01111000	X	01011000
l	01101100	L	01001100	y	01111001	Y	01011001
m	01101101	M	01001101	z	01111010	Z	01011010

This is called a binary representation of the English alphabet, and it uses only bits. The computer would then write the sentence "I saw a whale" as:

01001001   01110011 01100001 01110111   01100001
   [I]   [S]   [A]   [W]   [A]

01110111 01001000 01100001 01101100 01100101
   [W]   [H]   [A]   [L]   [E]

Cool, eh? How to create codes is one of the problems that intrigued Dr. Claude Shannon, an electrical engineer who was working for Bell Labs—the first company to produce telephones in the world. He invented a theory of information and this is why he appears in the stories of this book.

He told us that we can measure how much information a message contains, and that this information is the same no matter how the message is written!

Whether we write "I saw a whale" in English, or "j'ai vue une balaine" in French, we give the same amount of information.

A message has more information if it does not say something that we expect. For example, if you say "the sun will rise tomorrow," you do not give a lot of information; but if you say "there will be a solar eclipse tomorrow," then you are giving much more.

One of the many things Dr. Shannon explained is that all information could become bits, not just letters: images, music, everything we can measure can become bits. We can use bits not only to store information, but also to transmit information—this is what happens when you send a text message to your friends.

IF YOU LIKE TEXTING, YOU OUGHT TO LOVE HIM!

YOUR TURN!

WRITE YOUR NAME USING THE ASCII CODE:

READ WHAT THIS SAYS!
01000001 01001101 01000001 01011010 01001001 01001110 01000111

A BOOK HAS AROUND 200,000 CHARACTERS. HOW MANY BITS DO YOU NEED TO REPRESENT THIS BOOK USING THE ASCII CODE?

A BYTE IS A GROUP OF 8 BITS.
HOW MANY BYTES DO YOU NEED TO REPRESENT A BOOK WITH 200,000 CHARACTERS?

A USB STICK CAN STORE 4,000,000,000 BYTES (WHICH WE CALL 4 GIGABYTES). HOW MANY BOOKS CAN YOU STORE INSIDE IT?

IN A PLANET FAR FAR AWAY, THEY USE ONLY FOUR LETTERS: X, Y, Z AND W. CAN YOU MAKE A CODE THAT REPRESENTS EACH OF THE FOUR LETTERS WITH A UNIQUE GROUP OF BITS?

HOW MANY BITS DO YOU NEED FOR EACH LETTER?

CHAPTER 02
COMPRESSION

When we store information, we want to use the smallest space needed. This is like folding your clothes carefully so that you take out all the air, and you can store more clothes in your drawer.

COMPRESSION REMOVES REDUNDANCY— (PARTS THAT ARE NOT NEEDED).

Here is an example. You can write the following text message to your friend:

 "You are green in color!"
...or you can compress it and write, "You are green!"
...or you can compress it even more and write "U r green!"

The message that you send is always the same, but when you compress, you use fewer letters so you write it faster.

THE ENGLISH LANGUAGE HAS A LOT OF REDUNDANCY.

For example, many times we can remove all the vowels from a sentence, and still be able to understand what the sentence says!

Tr t d ths wth ths sntnc! s t vr dffclt r nt?

Thus, we could store only the consonants in the computer, and save space. The problem with this is that sometimes we may get confused. For example, if we write "mn" it can mean "man" or "mine" or "moon" or "mean"—we would not know...

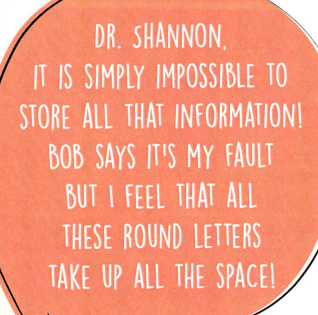

Shannon (and his colleague, Fano) came up with a more clever way to compress sentences, so that we can never get confused and still use a small number of bits. Note that in English sentences, the letters are not all used equally often.

People measured the letter frequency over many English texts and found that, in most texts with 100 letters, the letter "e" appears at least 12 times, the letter "o" at least 8 times, while other letters like the letter "z" are rare and appear less than 1 time.

This is why when you play hangman it is a good strategy to start guessing the letter "e," and why in scrabble, the letter "z" has a lot of points (there are very few words that use this letter).

In the ASCII (American Standard Code for Information Interchange) code we described in chapter 1, we always used 8 bits for each letter. Thus if we had 100 letters, we would need 800 bits to store it.

Shannon's idea was: what if we use fewer bits for the letters that appear very often, like the letter e, and more bits for the letters that appear very rarely, like the letter z?

Shannon showed that in this case, most texts with 100 letters can be represented with around 262 bits—much less than the 800 bits we had to use before!

We can do this, for example, by using the following code:

SYMBOL	CODE	SYMBOL	CODE	SYMBOL	CODE
e	010	l	10101	g	011001
t	1101	d	01101	b	011000
a	1011	c	00001	v	1100000
o	1001	u	00000	k	11000011
i	1000	f	110011	x	110000100
n	0111	m	110010	j	1100001011
s	0011	w	110001	q	11000010101
h	0010	y	101001	z	11000010100
r	0001	p	101000		

This is called the Huffman code.

Shannon also proved we cannot compress more than that… this is the best we can do. This "best we can do" is what Information Theory calls ENTROPY.

He showed that if we have something unknown (e.g. an unknown letter), the smallest amount of bits we need on average equals its entropy.

Today, we compress not only text, but also images, and videos. This allows us to save space, and thus store more on our devices. For example, if we compress photos, we can put 16 times as many photos inside the phone memory before we run out of space! This is a lot!

YOUR TURN!

IN AN OLD BOOK, SOME OF THE LETTERS ARE HALF ERASED. CAN YOU STILL READ THIS SENTENCE?

"ANGRY PEOPLE ARE NOT ALWAYS WISE."

WRITE YOUR NAME USING THE HUFFMAN CODE:

WHAT DOES THIS SAY?
01001 1001 1001 01101 110001 1001 0001 11000011

IS SHANNON RIGHT?
TAKE YOUR FAVORITE CHAPTER BOOK AND NOTE HOW MANY TIMES YOU SEE EACH OF THE ALPHABET LETTERS IN A PAGE (USING "A" AND "E" AS EXAMPLES):

```
A |||                L                    W
B                    M                    X
C                    N                    Y
D                    O                    Z
E ||||| ||           P
F                    Q
G                    R
H                    S
I                    T
J                    U
K                    V
```

Assume that in a far far away planet, the four letters they use occur with different frequency.

X is used most frequently, Y less frequently, Z even less frequently, and W very rarely.

Find a code that takes advantage of this, and uses fewer bits than the code you found in Chapter 1, for the following sentence:

YXZXXWXYX

What do you do if at school you want to tell a secret to a friend? How do you make sure nobody else overhears it?

Perhaps you whisper… or perhaps you write your message on a piece of paper that only your friend can see. Or say you are a spy, and you want to leave a secret message that only your team can understand—how can you do that?

Information security has exactly this goal: it looks at how we can transmit a message to a friend so that "an enemy," who may overhear the communication, does not learn what it is. We can do this by "ENCRYPTING" the message and having our friend decrypt it.

THIS IS CALLED A SECRET CODE.

Secret codes have been used for a long time.

For example, Julius Caesar used such a secret code for his army to exchange messages. The Caesar Code replaces each letter in the alphabet with a letter some places down the alphabet: If we shift by 2 letters, A would become C, B would become D, etc. For the last letters, Y became A and Z became B.

The message "Meet me in Rome" would then be written as:

OGGV OG GK TQOG

If we shift by 5 letters A becomes F, B becomes G, and the encrypted message becomes:

RJJY RJ NS WTRJ

This code is not hard to "break." We can simply try all possible shifts, and one of them will work, giving a meaningful sentence. We just need to do some computations and spend enough time!

We can similarly design codes when we transmit the binary representation of words. For example, we could say that we make all ones 0 and all zeros 1... but again, this is an easy code to break.

How can we design a code that cannot be broken—even if we try very hard to break it, even if we had infinite time? Even if an alien comes and can do all possible computations, and check all possible combinations very fast?

Shannon proved that to have an "unbreakable" code, Alice and Bob must share a "secret key," and use this secret key only once. This is a sequence of '0's and '1's that is as long as the message we want to transmit. Say that we have a message of ones and zeros to send, for example say that we use the ASCII mapping:

01010100 01101111 01100100 01100001 01111001

We have 5x8=40 bits to send.

The secret key, is a set of another 40 bits, that Alice and Bob have agreed on in advance—only they know it; Eve knows nothing about this secret.

For example, the secret key could be:

1100101 0010011 0111001 1001000 1110100

How do we use this secret key? We can just add, bit by bit, the secret key and the message. That is, add the first bit of the message with the first bit of the secret key, the second bit of the message with the second bit of the secret key, and so on...

... but how do we add bits?

We use an operation that is called "XOR" (pronounced *ex-or*), which is like an addition but has a funny property: a number xor itself is always zero!

$$1 \text{ XOR } 1 = 0 \quad 0 \text{ XOR } 0 = 0 \quad 1 \text{ XOR } 0 = 1$$

Alice uses this operation to combine the first bit of the message and the secret key, then the second, the third, until she combines all forty bits.

original message:
01010100 01101111 01100100 01100001 01111001

key:
11001011 00100110 01110010 10010001 11110100

encrypted message:
10011111 01001001 00010110 11110000 10001101

So now she has an ecrypted message. She sends this encrypted message to Bob. Bob, who also has the key, can reverse the operation: he takes the encrypted message, he xors it with the key again, and gets the original message! (the key cancels itself—because if we xor a bit with itself we get zero!)

xor key:
11001011 00100110 01110010 10010001 11110100

original message:
01010100 01101111 01100100 01100001 01111001

This way, even though Eve may receive the encrypted message, she will not understand it because she does not know what the key is!

The name "pad" comes because spies used this encryption method, and the keys were given to them in a pad of paper. Each sheet of the pad contained a different key, so as soon as the spy used one key, the top sheet could be easily torn off and destroyed.

As far as we know, the first time this technique was invented was in the 19th century. Shannon was the first to prove that this encryption cannot be broken, if we change the key every time!

WRITE A SENTENCE WITH 3-5 WORDS:

I Love you ~~to~~ to.

USE CAESAR'S CODE WITH A SHIFT OF TWO AND WRITE THE ENCRYPTED MESSAGE BELOW:

k ngxe ~~ka jw~~ vq

Alice sent another message to Bob!
Can you decrypt it and find what it says?
(To go from bits to letters, use ASCII.)

"10111000 00110000 10100000 00011000 00010110"

KEY: 11110000 01010101 11001100 01110100 01111001

THE FOLLOWING MESSAGE IS ENCRYPTED WITH CAESAR'S CIPHER—BUT YOU DO NOT KNOW EXACTLY WHAT SHIFT WAS USED. CAN YOU BREAK THE CODE AND FIND OUT THE MESSAGE?
"KSSH NSF!"

NOW TRY THIS:
"ULUHO TQO Y BYAU JE BUQHD IECUJXYDW DUM"

Hint:
How do people break codes? One way is to try all possibilities, but this may take too long! Another idea is to use the fact that letters do not appear with the same frequency. We had discussed before how we can use this for compression. We can use the same observation to break codes!

For example, the letter e is the most common letter in english. In the above sentence, the character that appears most times is u. So perhaps E was mapped to U! Try this—what shift would it correspond to?

CHAPTER 04
ERROR CORRECTION

You know how sometimes you try to talk to a friend in a noisy room and the friend cannot hear you—so you have to repeat what you said for your friend to understand?

This is a form of "error correction." The first time you talked there was an ERROR and you CORRECTED this error by repeating your message until your friend was able to understand.

You were the SENDER, your friend was the RECEIVER, and you communicated a message with the help of error correction.

This is what happens in this chapter: the letter A was sent in a noisy room, and came out garbled by the noise...

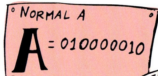

When we send bits, there can be noise, and some of the bit values can get flipped—some ones can become zeros and some zeros can become ones.

For example, to send the letter A, assume we use the ASCII code and send:

$$0100001$$

If the fourth bit value gets flipped, then the receiver gets 0101001 which corresponds to the letter Q!

So for the receiver to be able to understand correctly what we send, we need to be able to correct such errors.

The most straightforward way of error correction is to use
REPETITION.

Assume that a sender has 4 bits to send. The sender repeats these bits three times, so it sends 3x4=12 bits.

If only one error happens, the receiver can use a majority rule to decide what was send. That is, because there is only one error, at least two out of the three bits have to be correct. For example, assume the receiver gets:

$$0 1 0 1 0$$
$$0 0 0 1 0$$
$$0 1 0 1 0$$

Since the first bit is 0 all three times, we know its value has to be 0.

For the second bit, the receiver gets 1 twice, and 0 once—so the correct value must be 1.

The third and the fourth bits are also correct, so the receiver knows that the correct message is: 01010.

With this trick, we were able to correct one error—but instead of sending 4 bits, we send 12 bits.

We say that this is "a code of rate 4/12 = 1/3" because it needs to send 3 bits for each message bit.

What is not so great, however, is that it will take three times the time to send (or the space to store) the same message.

We can do better:

We can send 7 bits instead of 12 bits, and still be able to correct one single error. That is, we can use a code of rate 4/7—a higher rate than 1/3.

This is achieved by what is called the HAMMING CODE, invented by Dr. Richard Hamming.

This code takes four bits and converts them into seven bits—it adds three extra bits every four so that we can protect from one error.

The sender looks at what is the value of the four bits it has and, instead of repeating them three times, sends only three additional bits, as the following table shows:

ORIGINAL BITS	PARITY BITS
0000	000
0001	011
0010	101
0011	110
0100	110
0101	101
0110	011
0111	000
1000	111
1001	100
1010	010
1011	001
1100	001
1101	010
1110	100
1111	111

The four bits you want to send and the additional three bits are what we call the Hamming code.

What is special about this code is that any two 7-bit sequences differ in at least three bit positions, and thus if a single error happens we cannot confuse between any two of the sequences.

For example, if we receive the sequence 1101 111 then we know the sequence 1111 111 was sent.

So you can correct as much as you did repeating three times the same code, but you are sending much less.

Pretty cool eh? These extra bits are the PARITY bits Dr. Shannon gave to A to make sure she will not suffer the same fate again.

So, what if we want to correct two or more errors?

If you talk very fast, it is harder to hear you in noise. The same happens when you transmit bits—the faster you send them, the easier it is that bits are flipped, so correcting one error for every four bits may not be enough—or it may be too much. Maybe you now have an error every eight bits!

Shannon studied what is the smallest number of error correction bits we need to add. This determines the rate we can achieve, depending on how much noise we have. The more the noise, the smaller the rate, because we need a lot of error correction bits to send the message reliably. He found what is the maximum rate for a given amount of noise. He called this **THE CAPACITY**.

The capacity is how fast we can send information over a channel, correcting all bits that are flipped when we receive them at the other end. This means that if the code rate you use on a channel is above its Shannon capacity, you will not be able to fix the problem, no matter how hard you work—it would take a miracle!

Therefore, this is the fastest you can transmit bits on that channel reliably. Shannon's work started the area of **INFORMATION THEORY**, which today continues to study how we understand, process, store, and communicate information.

YOUR TURN!

Assume we want to send one bit, and we want to correct up to two errors. We want to use repetition to achieve this.

How many times do we need to repeat this bit, so that we are sure, no matter which two errors happen, we can always tell what the sender send?

What is the rate of the code?

WHAT IF NOW WE WANT TO USE REPETITION CODING TO SEND ONE BIT AND WE WANT TO BE ABLE TO CORRECT UP TO 3 ERRORS?

HOW MANY TIMES SHOULD WE REPEAT THE BIT? WHAT IS THE RATE?

CAN YOU SEE A TREND?
IF WE WANT TO BE ABLE TO CORRECT UP TO K ERRORS, HOW MANY TIMES DO WE NEED TO REPEAT EVERY BIT? WHAT IS THE RATE?

YOU WANT TO USE THE HAMMING CODE TO SEND THE FOLLOWING SEQUENCE:

11100 0110 101110 0010

WHAT ARE YOU GOING TO SEND?

Assume that there is this very strange channel, where if the sender sends A, then the receiver gets either A or B, but we don't know which one ahead of time.

It is like a coin flip that comes up either heads or tails, but we don't know which one will come up ahead of time.

Can you find a way to use this channel to send the sequence 10011 without making any error?

PUTTING THE PARTS TOGETHER

When you send a text message, all the operations we described before happen: the letters are first converted to bits (chapter 1), then compressed to remove redundancy (chapter 2), then encrypted so that no eavesdropper can learn your

message (chapter 3). It is then encoded with an error correction code (chapter 4) so that no mistake happens. At the receiver, the reverse operations happen before each letter appears on your friends screen.

ANNA SCAGLIONE
CHRISTINA FRAGOULI

Made in the USA
San Bernardino, CA
23 November 2017